'Victims of childho
survive. This book
lifetime of nightmares, depression, and suicide attempts.

Like millions of other adults who were molested as children, I was labelled a psychotic or mentally ill, placed on drugs, and offered a stay in a psychiatric ward. I am one of the fortunate few who was able to fight long enough and loud enough to find what I needed to help me out of despair.

We, as survivors, need your help. We need you to hear our gruesome stories, to believe the unbelievable. We need you to help us eliminate the secrecy and indifference that destroys the lives of one of every three little girls and one of every five little boys in your neighbourhood.'

Diane Ella Esther

Out of Incest & Abuse

A BOOK OF HOPE

Diane Ella Esther

EDITED BY JAMES STRECKER

Mini Mocho Press

Hamilton, Ontario

PUBLISHER'S NOTE: Since the publication of *Out of Incest, A Book of Hope*, both the title of the book and the author's name have changed. After discussing the poems during hundreds of workshops, Ms. Esther realized that the book, though specifically about incest, is also about every kind of abuse. She changed her name after ending her thirty-four year marriage.

Published by Mini Mocho Press, Jackson Station, Box 57424, Hamilton, Ontario, Canada L8P 4X2.

Cover photograph by James Strecker.

Fifth printing, 2006.

ISBN 0-921980-02-7

FOR YOU WHO GAVE ME LOVE AND LIFE:

For Jason, my Son Extraordinaire

For Mark, my Son Courageous

For James, my Mentor Gentle

For Ceri, Karen, Nancy, Donna, Pat, Susan, Jacqueline, Mary Jo, Kevin, Chris, Brenda, Geraldine, Wendy, Jeremy, Chris T., Leah, Kathy, Lon, Sylvia, Jean, Helen, Gary, Paul, Diane, Joyce, Greg, Jack, Leona, Teresa, Tracey, David, Penny, Ruth, Len, Julianna, Ross, Phyllis, Francine, Lee, Tom, Paulette, Margaret, Syd, Louise, Robert, Ted, Inez, Dorothy, Murray, and each Supporter, Friend and Survivor Precious.

MOLEST. A word of moderate impact. The Concise Oxford Dictionary tells us molest means 'meddle injuriously with a person.'

INCEST. An easy, mild word. Oxford describes incest as 'sexual intercourse between two persons regarded as too closely related to marry each other.'

An eleven year old victim of molestation and incest gives you her version:

I used to be normal
Plaid-lined forest-green coat, patent shoes to match
Pink cheeks. Fair hair. Bright smile.
Sunshine Yellow Life blooming.

Then my daddy filled me up
with shit.
That's what it felt like: shit.
Shall I show you how he did it?

Brackish portrait done vivid
too much detail
too much
living colour

living through Rape and Sodomy and Buggery
and swelling flesh entering a baby's body. No?
You want to see it? I don't want to live it.

I don't have a choice

Someone bigger than me
makes me look at it
every day
every day
every day

Someone bigger than me
paints me brown and flat
pins me to his canvas

Look at it, Ladies and Gentlemen
Look at it with me
Thirty years later
the pictures still play on my screen:

his body oozes over mine
like excrement
shit-caked hands cram their gruesome contents
into me
whole fistfuls of shit slather up my legs,
past pink vagina lips
splitting hymen not eleven years old

my stomach fills and swells, he licks
his lips and my breasts,
stained brown together

a gooey slick surrounds my heart
ta-boom, ta-boom, ta-
we hear a gurgle,
The Death Rattle,
I gag, I retch
he chuckles
greedy cheshire with wet lips, slobbering jaw
arching, writhing, burrowing

his bowels empty
into my cranium ...
eyes ... nostrils ... ears ...
every orifice plugging and
filling and
distending and distorting

overflow trickles
down cheeks that used to be
pink
used to be normal
Sunshine Yellow Life
painted brown by daddy's brush

The Living of Sex Abuse

Hit me, daddy
Hit ME
Don't hit my mommy
She's gonna die

Your face is all red
My tummy is scared
Mommy, Mommy, run away

It's OK now, Mommy
He's hitting me
Stay on the floor, Mommy

Mommy, you don't have to cry now
Please don't cry anymore

God
and
me
protect my Mom
till dark
when night gets through the cracks

I pray:
Dear God,
Keep out the night
Help me chase the devil
away from my Mom

But then it's dark
and devil-dark
The back door slams
and
Daddy's home

Night Monsters under my bed

But sometimes I make it
in three giant steps
Tangle the covers around
Curl up
safe

Sounds in the night
They shouldn't be there
Night Monsters?

Daddy pukes on the kitchen floor
Mommy leads him to bed
Closes their door in my face

Monsters
Night sounds
eat me alive
How much more could it hurt
if I died?

Cooking eggs, playing banjo,
reading Uncle Wiggley:
memories of my Grandpa Bop

Listen to Daddy stumble home drunk
I'm safe in the good times,
safe with Bop

Mom's face hits the floor
but I won't see her bleed.
Squint up my eyes and remember:

'Soft boiled with ketchup, Bop!'
'You've got it honey. Comin' up!'

Do what Mom says, kiss Daddy hello,
smell the vomit, taste the salt.
Hold my breath and recall:

'Play "Oh Dem Golden Slippers," Bop!'
'You betcha! All twenty-nine verses for you!'

Mom and Dad in the bedroom
I can't hear Mommy cry and moan.
Pick out a favourite story:

'Read Uncle Wiggley just once more, Bop!'
' "… if the blueberry doesn't fall …" '

The girl in our house
plays mommy
while Herbie gets to play
somewhere down the road

Daddy's getting up,
the big bear
rumbles out of his cave

You never noticed me before
You never touched me
Daddy, why are you shaking?

Fat little sausage fingers,
dirty fingernails
on my breasts,
tiny breasts, starting to grow
at last

Now I want to cut them off.
Ugly little bumps.

Don't be gentle,
it makes me feel loved.
I know you don't look at me
with love

Shovel your fingers deep
Harder   Harder
Dig your filthy nails far inside,
rip me to pieces, throw me away

No tenderness, please.
Make my body bleed.
Inside, outside, bleed
I never want to feel anything. Never.

I hope inside you'll apologize
I hope I'll forgive
and we'll live happily as never before.
Then you call me back to your chair.

flowers on the bedspread under us
count them
swirls and patterns
colours all melt together

he is naked
beside me he is naked
he is taking my clothes off
slowly
slowly while I try to stare over his body
at anything beyond

no
no, I don't want to look at it
no, I don't want to touch it
no!
but I'm not supposed to say no to daddy
only my mind says no
I say no inside

it doesn't matter
it doesn't matter anyway
I always do as I'm told

there isn't a part of me left clean
now I have to touch and rub his huge thing
no
no, I won't use the right word for it
the right word would make it real
and I need to pretend

my hands hold and pet your naked body
the dirt under your nails
spreads to mine

I clean myself off in the bathroom
slimy
dirty
I try not to look in the mirror
but I see myself in the mirror
I spit at my face

Every day
begins with smiles for Mom,
ends with smiles and hugs from Dad

I stay in the kitchen, you come after me,
there are no safe rooms in our house
Can't anyone help me?

Another attack,
grinding from behind into me,
I try to escape in a book
propped up in front of me

Thirty times,
forty times, over and over,
sentences glimpsed but not read

The book slides out of my grip,
the explosion rocks us,
yanks me back to the bed
Daddy!

Slamming harder and harder against me,
moaning,
pushing like never before,
Our Little Secret, you call it.

1952 | JUST DESSERTS

Clean it up, Ella!
I said CLEAN IT UP!

He kicks her into the sticky mess,
sugar and milk he's poured
on the floor.

Mom is mopping
 mopping
 mopping
Her life depends on it.

Grandma's eyes find mine.
She shakes her head from side to side,
and I stare at the butcher's knife
in my hand. Could I have used it?

'You're enjoying that,
aren't you, honey?'

No, daddy! No, I'm not!
No. It's my body, not me.
I hate it when your fingers
make me move this way.

Please
don't make me like this.
Please
don't make me want this.

My body is dirty,
dirty like you.
God. Mommy. Forgive me.

They give us a book to read in Health Class.
Some of the girls laugh at the pictures.

I know what 'it' looks like.
I know what 'it' feels like.
I know.

I see 'it' even when you do it from behind.
Eyes squinted half-closed.
Nose all scrunched up.
Mouth open half way.

You sigh and quiver and shake all over.
I feel that too, when you jab at me with 'it'.

But Daddy, I got an 'A' on the Health test.
I know what some of the girls don't know.
I think I'm pregnant.

Mom?
A girl should tell her Mother
everything, shouldn't she?
I think I'm going to have a baby.
You see, Daddy's been....

Diane, are you sure you're not
making this up? ... Honey?

1954 | CONSPIRATORS

he's never Dad
Daddy
or Your Father
anymore

only he
him
or harry
in small letters

and I'm never alone with
'him'
anymore

to the world
we are Mother and Father
Sister and Brother
The Loving Family

hugs and kisses abound
smiles show the world
All Is Well

God, You've seen fit
to reward me at last.
I'm going to teach Sunday School!
Grandma? Where's Mom?
Darn! Still in bed.

Peek through the doorway.
Shadows. Movement. Bodies together.
Not in their separate beds.
He covers her naked body.
He drools over her.
Oh, Mom!

He's doing it to her.
Wasn't I enough?
You had to take my Mother too?
How could you let him?
Close the door. Lock it out.

I vomit my stomach and brain
in the toilet together.
'Diane. Honey. Open the door.
You don't know what he does to me.
He tears off my clothes. He's an animal.
You don't think I enjoy it?'

We never cry for Diane again.
Only dry tears for Diane. No tears.
We only cry for Mother.

too much time alone
lets me think
think
think
about 'him'

I have to pretend I love 'him'
pretend we're normal

so 'he' won't get mad
and 'he' won't beat up
Mom again

Mom sacrifices herself
for me
every night:
for me and my sins

Mom says
'he'd' track us down
and kill us if we left
if 'he' knew I told on 'him'

We have no choice
because of me and my sins

My sadness fits Mom
better than it fits me
I'll work the rest
of my life
to take it from her eyes

'This is wonderful, Diane,
I'm very proud of you.'

Oh, Miss Nelson, do you
really mean my story's good?
I'm good?
Oh! I'm sorry, God,
I didn't mean to act
conceited.

But Words, Words
I climb into them
No one can follow me
It's my own world
The one place I'm safe

Today, a love story:
I'm the heroine,
I love Him intensely,
He's severely burned
in a raging fire,
loses His mind,

I dedicate my life to caring
for Him,
We live happily ever after.

That's the sound
of Mom's quiet cries;
'he's' doing it to her again

Keep my hand over my mouth,
don't let it escape,

pull more blankets and covers up,
more pillows to muffle the noises
smashing my ears

and pray:
'Dear God,
don't let "him" hurt her
anymore.
Please don't punish me like this.

I know I'm filth
to touch myself, my body,
that way.
"he" taught me how, "he" made
my body squirm and enjoy it.

I'll never do it again;
just don't kill me this way.'

1955 | FIRST LOVE

Dear Diary:

I'm in love!

His name is Barry,
the family that lives
by the pond
across the bridge.

Barry is different,
quiet and shy like me.

We were all down at the lake
this aft
and the guys started chasing
the girls
to throw them in.

Barry started heading
my way
and I ran like the wind.

Then he caught me,
picked me up like a handful
of straw
(you know how skinny I am)

He made me feel so precious,
my heart beat wild,
I wanted time to stop

Oh, Barry, you do care, don't you?
It's not just another make-believe?

Everything jumbled together.
Can't tell where a memory ends
and another begins.
Tangled together, swirling
through my brain.
Can't let it out, gotta keep it in.

Somebody help me quick!
It's slipping, slithering through holes,
vomiting, green, lumpy, smelly,
memories …

Daddy's hands … other hands … many hands
Daddy … penis … another penis
Pictures afloat … memories … surrounded
Scare … Scare … Scare

Feel it … touch it … rub it
Bushes … cousin Doug … commanding
Pulses pound … his … mine
Scare … Scare … Scare

On a lap … hugs … cuddling
Grampa Jimmy … fingers … inside
Held up high … slowly lowering … on top of it
Scare … Scare … Scare

At a table … hands below … skirt aside
Can't refuse … Minister … tea party
Rubbing thighs … higher still … smile polite
Scare … Scare … Scare

Leering … stark naked … penis
My backyard … neighbour's son … waves
Run away … stay indoors … safe?
Scare … Scare … Scare

From high hopes to rock bottom.
I sway back and forth.

He loves me.
He loves me not.
He loves me.
Please let him love me, God.

I've had all my love stored up
inside
all my life.
I need to give it to someone,
use it on someone.

If I do as I'm told, I'm good.
If I'm good, I'll be loved.
If I'm loved, I'll be valuable.

But I do as I'm told!
Please let him love me, God.

Barry's gone. Drifted away.
I thought I deserved him.
And love.
Presumptuous, wasn't I?

Well, Mom was right again.
She always says, 'The meek shall
inherit the earth.' She says,
'When we get high and mighty
and better than others,
we get knocked right back down.
Where we belong.'

Well, I'm here again, Lord. At the bottom.

I'm learning, though. Learning slowly.
I don't walk up to life
straight ahead
anymore.

I ease into it, sidle up to it.
Flinching.
Waiting to see what it will slip me this time.

I've been training myself
to tiptoe in,
not approach it head-on,
a sideways shuffle,
then I scamper back.
Before anyone notices me.

'Well, I've only been cooking
for twenty years, honey,
but if you think you can show me
a better way,
you go right ahead.'

The smirk appears
and I split down the middle again.
One side of me wants to apologize.
The other side wants to yell:

'Listen to me!
I want to show YOU something
for a change. Just once!'

Guilt. Anger. Anger. Guilt.

But don't try to tell Mother.
Mother's ideas are the only Good Ideas.

Mother. Bruises on your arms,
dressing gown draped low, marks
run down like little blue mice,
slither down your arms
into my heart.

Why do you let them show?
You mustn't know they hurt me.
You're reassuring me
that you're willing
to endure his fist
just for me.

Guilt. Guilt. Guilt.

How could I forget my books again?
Mom says my mind is 'Elsewhere.'
So do my teachers. They're all pretty close.

It tries to be anywhere but present.
That's what I fight for everyday.

Take it from the 'here' and the 'now',
use the tricks Mom taught me
when I was little:

'Don't cry, honey.
Try not to think about it.
Next week we'll go to grandma's.
You'll pick berries
and put them on your cereal.
We'll have a good time.
That's a good girl. Think of all
the good things to come.
Forget about the bad parts.

Give me a big smile.'

So I cram it in …
'Back of the brain, please. Move it along.
Make room.'

1957 | SHAME

The rumblings start slowly
Pressure building
Stewing
Boiling
Finally the explosion

Neighbours and friends come running
to see. 'What happened, what was that boom?'
'Oh, it's just Diane Howard. Her brain exploded.'
'NO!' My God! Look, over there, bits
and pieces of her all over the yard!
There's more, there!
Putrid! Garbage!

Is that what she's had inside?
Carrying that around all these years?
Poor dear.
Imagine,
living and walking and talking
with all that crap in her pretty little head.
And nobody knew.
Why didn't she say something?'

'You know, I always thought there was something
strange in that family.'

'Oh well, it's over and done with now.'

'What a shame. And she was so cute.'

A new job offer.
He tells me I'm a smart cookie.
I can handle it.

I stand taller,
shoulders filling. Positive. Starched.

Yes, I'd like an interview.
Yes, I'm interested in the position.
I think I can do it, I'm bursting
to take the chance!

That's your cue.

A pinhole of Scare,
air escapes, I'm deflating.

'Damn Scare, you follow me everywhere!'

'But I give you an excuse.'

'I can't move!'

'Exactly … no moves, no failures.'

'Mommy, Mommy, Mommy, Mommy.
I'm sorry.
I failed again'

I hope ours will be more than a marriage.
I'll be more than a wife.
I want to be your partner.
I want you to share everything with me.
All of your happiness or burdens.
All the joys and sorrows.
Always.

I always want to be your lover.
I hope our love will always have
the excitement and passion it has now.
That instead of dying, it will
grow stronger and stronger
as time goes on.

I'll be a good mother to our children.

1963 | PERFORMING

Mom says she held me in her arms
and told me: 'Someday
you'll know this feeling, Diane,
the supreme love and devotion
a Mother alone can feel,
complete joy, life's final purpose.'

And now the doctor's telling me
God is going to take my baby away.

If it's defective, I'll lose it.
If there's nothing wrong with it,
I'll keep it.
That's what he means, isn't it?

Then I'll hold on all the way to my toes.
God will make it heal,
He'll see that it's perfect. Tiny
fingers and toes. Beautiful
baby of mine.

Pretend this route leads to freedom,
the end of the circus. Life
will be perfect 'when I become a mother.'

Al. Carry me. I'm so tired,
tired and scared. What if I lose the baby?
All my reasons will die with it,
my reasons to live.
I can't take things in stride.
I was never taught how.

1964 | FIFTY-FIFTY

I'm an expert in the art of camouflage.
I keep one part of me hidden.
The world hasn't seen the real Diane.

she's still very young, my little girl.
she knows all my fears and sadness.

she cried gently in my head as 'he'
rubbed my body against his: 'Oh, God.
please don't. Mommy, Mommy, help her/us.
don't look, Diane, close your/our eyes.
pretend. get away from here, quick.
shut your/our mind. good girl. we're gone.'

she helped me hide from Mom's bruises:
'It's okay, Diane. I'm here. turn your/our
eyes away. don't look at them. see outside
it's snowing. let's go skating.'

she knows I still believe in the childish
verse: 'step on a crack, you'll break
your Mother's back.' I still avoid cracks.

she cries with me when I make mistakes:
carrots aren't cooked; gravy's lumpy again.
Al teases.

'You're right, Diane. His
sarcasm hurts a lot. You smile for Al,
I'll cry inside for you/us.'

I'd be so alone if I didn't have her,
nobody else could love the real me.
The me who hates. Who screams.
Who touches my own body. Some day
I'd like us to be a whole person,
all one instead of half and half.

I am divided:

This me knows Al's kidding	This me is hurt and cries
This me says it's childish verse	This me jumps the cracks
This me sees the bruises	This me skates away
This me turns 20, 21, 22	This me stays 13

Scolded without a word.
The eggs are too hard, he
bounced his knife on them.
His unspoken words: You can't
do anything right. When will you learn?

I do try, Al. I jump for the milk
when you stir your tea, hand you the sugar
before you reach for it. Shouldn't
that count for something?

I keep my mind aware, On Alert, just for you,
but so many years I've been trying to use
only half of it. Now I'm letting it open
again and the cracks widen
and naked memories spill out.

I try to be selective, sort the good
from the bad. Not that one! Push it back,
quick! OK, let this one through, it's safe.
Oh, no! Another black chunk. Slam it shut!
Enough for today. Enough.

Working at it, day after day, I feel a
million years old. Wish I could let you see
what life is like inside your Diane.

'He' holds Jason against his unwashed chest,
nicotined fingers wrapped around
a tiny leg. Stinking fingers
that once raked into my vagina.

My mind screeches: 'DON'T TOUCH HIM!'

I'll slash, rip apart your chest, bury
my hands in flesh to reach the thumping
heart inside. That black walnut, shrivelled,
hard, immobile now. I'll assure it won't
beat again. Won't pound against anyone
else's body. Won't lead your warped
mind to destroy other lives.

I hiss at 'him': 'DON'T!'

The mother bear rescues her cub; the
predator knows enough to back to safety.
I cradle my precious son, croon and
console him, he has been in the arms
of death. I promise to God

and the child, his grandfather will die
before 'he' touches him again.

Doctor told me my little Mark has brain damage.

Mark can't run like the others
because I let him live in my womb,

Can't work his fingers normally
because I fought to give him life,

Can't speak as well, pump a swing,
ride a bike, bounce a ball,
because I wouldn't say,
'Let him die.'

Forgive me, Mark.
I fought for you and now you have to pay for it.

Hold tight, my beautiful boy.
Cling to your mother.

You won't have to fight alone.

It's time to play my Ace-in-the-Hole.
I have to kill you.
I have to kill myself.

My life goes on without me.
I'm missing.
Arms move, lips keep smiling but
it's all a facade.
My friends don't know I'm gone,

they never really knew I was here,
I've deceived them all.
Wife. Friend. Mother. None of the
titles fit. Not even the number
zero: never was, never will be.

Al, Help me.
Hold me tonight while I cry.
When will you realize how useless
I am? And ask me to leave?

'That's not true, Diane. You are
a good wife and mother. You
look after us, sew our clothes,
make a home, have Christmas dinners.
We all love you. Why can't you feel
good about yourself?'

I don't know.

'Don't let these things bother you.'

But Albert, there is no switch in there.
I don't turn it on, I can't shut it off.

'I'm getting tired of supporting your
fight, Diane.'

Sorry, Al.

Worthless. No good. Junk.
Even my own father used me
and threw me away.

I have to tell 'him' I remember.
I know what 'he' did to 'his'
little girl.

'But, Diane, you know how violent
"he" can get. "He'll" take it out
on me if you talk to "him".
Please don't do this to me.'

You're right, Mom.
I won't say a word to 'him'.
Sshh, sshh, it's all over.

We cry together again –
for Mom.

1968 | A.M.

A new design
to the wallpaper.
Pie crust in chunks slides down to the floor.

Is this, then, the edge?
The last inch of safe ground
before the pit?

A simple task
and I can't succeed,
can I be worth saving?

Give it up, Diane.
Enter that womb of blackness, fall into it,
down, down to oblivion.
So enticing. Gone the tightropes and tears.

Pills, medicine chest.
Can I down enough? How many will it take?
Mark. I'll have to crush his.
Mix them with his juice.
Oh, God.
Oh, Al, no.
Oh, Mommy, no.

Not my beautiful Mark. Somebody save my baby.

Telephone. Straight ahead. Focus. Dial.
Dear friend Phyllis. Save them.
Come and take my children.
I finally did it ... I made it all the way
to crazy.

Swallow hard. Again. The vomit
is still so close. The words taste
rancid and bitter.

'he' molested me.
My own father did it to me
and now I'm telling this man. A man
who has a penis. Does he do it
with his daughter?

Maybe he wants me to talk about it
so he can fantasize
as he rubs it against
his daughter's legs.

No.
I've got to trust him. There is no
other choice. Al is counting on me
to get better. Is there magic in
this chair? Yes.

He says there's a reason for my insanity.
'he' did it to me. 'he' made me worthless
and empty. Silent messages screamed at me
from 'his' shaking fat fingers … 'You are
nothing. YOU ARE NOTHING!!'
How meekly I accepted them.
I am flat.

My body, my ego, my mind,
all flattened by my father's vile touch.

'The kids say I only
have half a brain, Mommy.'
His eyes follow me, tearing my heart.
One day there'll be too many cracks
to repair. My beautiful boy.

I'll fend off the world, find only
the good people in it for you.
Surround you, fence you in with me.
We'll pick out the good parts,
shut out the sad.
Choose our own pictures.

You won't miss the world.

New Programmes, New Diagnosis,
New Social Workers, New Disabilities.
New Titles: Learning Disabled
                  Minimal Brain Disfunction
                  Cerebral Palsied
                  Retarded

I'm not supposed to hold your hand?
Or provide a buffer for you
on your way through life?

Controlling.
Overprotective.
Yes, I've been labelled too. Yet
warning sirens scream at me: DO SOMETHING
                                        STEP IN
before history repeats itself.
You've lived your lifetime on the brink;
don't let him walk alone.

My Grandfather warned me
when I was just sixteen:
    'Anyone can handle a crisis, Diane.
    It's the everyday living
    that will kill you.'
You hit the nail on the head with that one,
didn't you, Bop?

Never still, never think, always run.
To be still is to think. To think is suicide.

Sherry found her way out with it.
I watched her family crumble afterwards.
Would mine miss me that way?

Sherry thought she was no good for anything,
too. I couldn't make Sherry listen.
I heard her children cry
when she was buried.

Mom comes for tea, sips
gently and spins
a real-life fairytale.

In 1934, she was pregnant
with my father's child.
He was seventeen, she nineteen.

His mother wouldn't give
permission to marry, so
Ella was locked away;

a bobsled accident
covered her absence
from the world.

She was whisked off
to hospital
in the dead of night

and ten days later
she came home with her
baby boy. The family decided

that her married sister
would adopt him, raise him
as my cousin Doug.

No BANG! No drums
or dramatic sound effects:
I am thirty-four, Herb

is twenty-eight, and we
have just been given
a forty-year-old brother.

Mom chokes on sobs:
'Do you look at me as a whore,
honey? I'm so dirty and filthy.

I gave away my first-born.
I didn't want to, I loved him
so. My perfect baby boy.

I nursed him and rocked him
ten whole days. He was part
of my body. The only thing

truly mine in the world. I was
simply a girl whose only mistake
was being born in 1914.'

Game of the Week:
Puke down Daddy's back

Daddy's arms around me
Hairy arms, hairy like
steel wool
Soft and gooey underneath
A dagger tattoo

Daddy's chest
Diane's chest
'Hi, honey,' says Daddy
Diane can't breathe
Can't get air

I catch Al's eye
I pretend to vomit
Down Daddy's back
Down Daddy's flannel shirt

It's soft and ordinary
Covered with puke he cannot see

The report from my psychiatric testing:
'Patient is in touch with reality; has
superior intellect; unable to make use
of it due to childlike emotions.'

Now what do I do? Grow up?
That's a little difficult at age
thirty-six while the beast of depression
looms in front of me every morning.

Wife
Mother
Can't bear the repeats of
yesterday and yesterday and yesterday
Where can I go, who can I see,
how can I escape? My list is endless:

Part time job as bookkeeper
Volunteer at Jay's school
Scorekeeper for Mark's bowling league
Riding lessons for Mark
Ceramics for me
Investigate programmes and schools
Sick Kids' Hospital for tests
Sessions with Psychiatrist

It's not enough. It'll never be enough.
I'm still disgusted at my laziness.
I disgust myself.

1977 | COMPANY'S COMING

Car pulls up
people spill out
hugs and kisses all around

'Hi, Diane.'
His arms reach out.

My teeth clench hard into numbness,
a word grinds out: 'Don't.'

His eyes lock into mine
His arms reach out again

'I said, "Don't." '

Last week he called my abuse
'lessons in sex education.'
And today, thirty-seven years late,

before Auntie, Uncle, Al, Mom, and God
I say the four letter word:
'Don't.'

My silence ends today.

I'm still a figment of my imagination
Can I convince the world
I exist,
a capable human being?

'Who, Diane?
Oh, she's kind and gentle and clever.
Very nice. You'd like her.'

But what if
I can't repeat that 'A' on my essay?
But what if
I can't fool the Professor again?

If I continue my classes,
Al and Dr. S. and the world
will find out
what I've always known:
I have no brains.

I do exist:
a thirty-nine-year-old dropout.

'Your Honour,
I wish to act as my own attorney.

Perhaps I can be freed from this
trap I've built. Having completed
several years of therapy, I'm
beginning to see the good qualities
of Diane we haven't recognized
before: cleverness, kindness ...'

'MRS. MATTIUSSI! ARE YOU NOT IN
CONTEMPT OF COURT? ARE YOU
NOT LYING NOW?'

Jerked back to reality. Slugged in
the stomach by my 'other secret',
this one all mine,
the one secret I have buried
even deeper than memories of savage
hands and sweaty bodies:

me cruelly flinging my little boy
down in his crib. Snarling. Smacking
his little bottom in a rage. Ignoring
his cries, his sobs, his arms.
'Don't make me look at this, your honour.'

'THE TRUTH, MRS. MATTIUSSI.'

Our battles began at nap time. His
screams jolted my body upright.
'Get to sleep! Now! No, you're not
getting up. Jason, lie down.
Mommy said, "DOWN!" '
I smack.

I smack and dribbles wet his chin.
One to get his attention.
One more to discipline.
One more in anger.
Again in anger.

'Your Honour, we find the defendant
guilty as charged. We sentence her
to life at hard labour.'

Thirty years, forty, fifty … hiding
the shame … I hit my child in anger.
I'll never forget,
I'll never forgive,
court is adjourned,
I do not appeal the decision.

Assertiveness Training.
The leader said it's OK
to talk about the bad parts.
How can this be? I've spent
forty years hiding from them.

Swear at them. Swear? Swear!
Curse them. Stand up.
My turn. FUCK OFF!
Good God. I said it.

I'm learning 'techniques'.
I'm. . . .

Mom's voice drifts in again,
'Nobody likes a pushy
little girl, Diane.'

But I'm tired of leaning backwards.
Is that you, Mom? I have to stop
listening now.
Something new is happening, someone
is teaching me to look after myself,
I'm stepping

into another world.
I'm an astronaut, daring
to peek into the Milky Way,
galaxies to discover,
aliens to greet. Just my guts
luring me on. The reward may be worth
the risk.

Later, at home,
Al, Jason, and Mark
all snicker across the table. A sarcastic
remark, said in fun, cuts through
me again.

My heart rate doubled, hands damp,
body quivering,
I try out my new formula from class:
Step 1: Al, when you tease me, my feelings get hurt.
Step 2: That makes me angry.
Step 3: Will you please not do that anymore?
Step 3A: I cannot and will not live in a home where
my feelings are not important.

His rebuke explodes in my face: 'Don't use that
assertiveness shit on me, Diane!'

Hours later, all talked out,
he holds me tight.

DAMN YOU, MOM!
You say to be a good girl and smile
and everyone will love me. But you
just want to show how good a mother
you are. So I stay sweet and let the world
walk on me, let them use me for a doormat.

DAMN YOU, MOM!
You say you are helping me, protecting
me from Daddy. But you are just scared
to leave. So you keep me tied to you, keep
me mired in the muck with you.

DAMN YOU, MOM!
You say not to cry over sadness, or be
mad about disappointments. But you
teach me to cry for you. So I learn
my feelings are not important.

DAMN YOU, AL!
You say you are happy I'm finding
myself. But you put up walls
and stop me when I confront your anger.
So I back off.

DAMN YOU, AL!
You say you understand if I need
time to myself. But
you growl if dinner is late. So I
put me last again.

They both carry a double-edged sword.
Dare I attack them? Duel with them,
Mom and Al? Safe in my group, I beat
pillows, I beat them, and challenge them.
Scream. Accuse. Free myself.

No! I won't look at your bruises, Mom.
No! I won't cry for you anymore.

No! I might not be home for dinner, Al.
No! I refuse to do laundry on Mondays.

At forty-two I finally live my rebellious
teens. I turn 15, 18, 20 years old.
I get angry.

The first time I was born
I exploded from Mother's body.
This time I am my own birth.
Assertiveness training, a language
foreign to me: re-parenting,
safety for self, feedback, taking
your own power.... More!! More!!
I'm addicted.

Week 5: Mom. Blame Mom. But she was
protecting herself, she didn't think
she was hurting me. How can I accuse her?
Good intentions, but my hell. Get off
that pedestal, Mom!

Week 10: I'm different, completely
someone else. I don't care about Mom,
about life, about my family. I'm not
depressed, just sitting 'outside' of my
feelings. My feelings are on hold.

Week 18: I don't want to make anyone happy.
Not my responsibility. I can say I don't
want to talk, with no excuses. I don't
have to be sugary and nice. I can tell
Mom to fuck off. I want to. No I don't.
I just don't want more obligation.
Write her off totally.

Week 18: Anger. 'harry'. Anger. It's more
about Mom than 'harry'. I don't hate her,
just don't want to be bugged anymore.
I'm not Miss Goody Two-Shoes. Hear that,
Mom? Don't bug me!

Week 20: She has to be the winner. Always.
She lies to make herself look good. Always.
I HATE THE SON OF A BITCH! But I mean the
old man. No, it's Mom I hate. She can't
listen, never has. All this time I thought
she was so perfect.

Week 21: No anger to 'harry'. Honest. I feel
sorry for the little boy, neglected, abused,
no chance to grow up. Couldn't give when he
became my father.
Now close my eyes, imagine his face, imagine
how he made me feel.... 'You made me feel
dirty. Cheap. You shouldn't have done that
to a little girl. You BASTARD! You made me
feel filthy. YOU SON OF A BITCH! Why did
you do it? BASTARD! I trusted you!'

Week 24: I'm speaking to a picture of little
girl Diane. You're cute and vulnerable, alone.
Fighting for your life, nobody on your side.
What an awful way to live. Such a lonely soul.
How could you do that, harry? You ruined
her life. You BASTARD! Her whole life. I'll
never forgive you. But it's my life you
ruined. She is me. You took away my childhood.
You gave me not skipping, but sex; not
marbles, but molesting. I need to kill you!
Stab you! Drive a knife through your heart
like you did to me! You cut me open, left
me bleeding in little shreds. All my life!

I was Diane, your little girl. I needed a daddy. I needed your love. But you gave me fingers up my body. My tiny body. You ass-hole, you piece of shit, you'll never touch anyone else! Knife! Knife in your face, in your chest, in your balls!

Week 30: Does anyone see changes in Diane?
'Your voice is stronger. You're more energetic. Brighter.'
'You're more in control. In charge. You look happier.'
'Younger. Pretty. You are present.'
'Your hair. Flower in your lapel. You have a right to please yourself.'

Our name says it all,
Adults Molested As Children.

Each of us digs back
to discover the source
of infection

Dig   Dig   Dig
Unearth revelations
I can learn   I can love   I am loved
I deserve to be here

In this room
In this world
In this life

Take my very own spot

Do you believe that, Diane?

Almost
I still need to talk to me
Powerful   powerful I am … the words
sink through my pores
dissolve in my bloodstream

antibiotics for my soul

I didn't know this was possible
I set 'my own agenda' here, lead
my own way. CONFRONTATION,
my final step of recovery.

I will give it all back
to Mom and Dad.

'I only did what I thought was best, Diane.'
Yes, but it was warped, Mom.
Rehearsals in the Group, role play,
pillows to beat. I have to be ready
for guilt and anger and sadness.

I study every book on the shelf,
write in journals,
cram for my finals.
I book my flight, my brain has
one track: CONFRONTATION.

I have to do this. Give it all back. Live.

1984 | TELEPHONE CALL

I'm calling for a reason
I'm flying out on Saturday
You and Mom and I
have to talk about forty-four years,
forty-four years I've tried
to hold my head together,
forty-four years of secrets
and lies and curtains pulled
over everything that was rotten
I think it's time our family
talked about these things

No dad, it's not my imagination
No dad, you can't deny it again

1984 | FLIGHT

Excess baggage I carry
on board today will not
fly home with me

A suitcase, my mind, crammed
with doubts, fears, guilt,
mind and bone-crushing sadness.
Anger. Hatred.

All will be left on the airport
carousel, unclaimed.

I am confident.
I can do it.
I am doing it.

Forty-four years
of solitary confinement,
I'm about to open the shackles
of my lifetime.

D-Day.
Count down with me.
Minutes, only minutes, till freedom.
I have taken the keys from my jailors.

Every day I gave you, my child, hell:
'Why don't you stay in and peel the
potatoes?' Because 'he' would never
get the dinner going. I gave you hell
every day, then one day you said,
'Mom, I can't come in the house.' And
you told me why. My heart broke. Absolutely broke.
'he' could do this to my daughter?
I had to protect my daughter and my
mother was away. So I went to HIS Mother!
And she said, 'I'm not a bit surprised
at what my son will do. But if you let
him know that you know, he'll kill her.
Just go back to work and watch her.'
Watch her! I had to go to work. So I
put a lock on your door and said,
'Diane, if I'm not here, honey, just
lock yourself in and don't let him near
you.' But one day you had the measles,
and I didn't have money for the bus
so I walked home. And I died all over
again. He was lying on the bed with you,
supposed to be telling you a story!
I told Nana, his mother, again, and she
said, 'She'll get over it.' But you were
changing and I knew you'd never forget
it. And I had ulcers so bad I was
terrible sick, but I went to work anyway.

And the doctor said, ‘How could you live
through it? How could your daughter live
through it? Do you want a psychiatrist?’
But in those days, if you went to a
psychiatrist, people thought you were
crazy and they put you in a home. So
I didn’t go. I should have gone. I
should have gone and got help. But my
mother said, ‘Those psychiatrists
only twist your mind more.’ And I’ve
lived with that, day after day after
month after years. He’s ruined my
life since I married him.

ME, RUIN YOUR LIVES?!
I haven't come here to ruin
anybody's life. I have come
to save my own. All the bad
things, all the crap, got stuffed
away in a closet. MY STOMACH WAS
THE CLOSET! I wanted to talk about it
but you wouldn't let me. You begged
me, 'Don't do this, Diane. Please.
You know he'll hurt me.' So I cried
for you. FOR YOU! And I was going crazy.
I thought God was punishing me for
my mortal sin, for masturbating. I
thought I would have to kill myself
and Mark too. Because if I couldn't
make it in this world, I felt he'd
never make it. Well, I'm not going to
rescue you from your side anymore.
You were an adult with choices.
I was a child, I was given no choices.
I went where I was told, did what I
was told. I had to go along with what
I was told. I now have choices. I have
chosen to say, 'NO MORE!'

I've said that I did it, I had my hands
where I shouldn't have. I regretted it.
I've prayed. I am going to leave. I only
need three thousand dollars and the truck.
Mom won't have to put up with me anymore.
I can't go see a psychiatrist. I could
never go to one. What would I say to this
person? I can't even talk about it with
you. And he's a stranger. You say you've
been in therapy for twelve years. Mom
and I don't have too many years left.
Maybe there's no point in starting. It's
a bit late now. We want some good times
before we die. But from here on in
there's a barrier between Mom and me.

No, we won't talk about weather
and bowling today. You will listen
to me. We will get things out
instead of burying them and causing
so much pain in my life.
Do you know what your molesting did
to me? It made me feel worthless,
useless, less than a whore. 'Cause
you would have paid a whore. And you
want me to feel better because you
never raped me completely, because you
only did it from the rear? WHAT THE
HELL'S THE DIFFERENCE? An eleven-year-
old girl was VIOLATED! TRAUMATIZED!
And I have been paying the consequences
for forty-four years. So I don't give
a SHIT if you run away! I don't give
a SHIT if you go for therapy! I just want
you to know I am finished with
secrets and lies.

Tuesday Night Group ...
'I did it! I feel terrific!
To hell with coffee, come
hear how I feel:

Can't get the words out fast enough.
As soon as the words are out of my
mouth, they're wrong. Obsolete.
The billionth of a second it takes
to pronounce the word is too long.
It's over before the speaking of it.
The life I see is sharp. Like when
I got new glasses, everything goes
from hazy to too bright. And the
instant I say the light is bright,
it changes to something else.
I'm taller and higher and larger
than everybody. I'm here in group
and suddenly I'm growing and rising
to the ceiling, and by the time I
realize I'm going up, that isn't it
anymore, there's another description:
I sit there and I look at their faces
and I'm flabbergasted that this is me,
that I'm not them. I don't even see me
the way I was before. I'm new. I'm
almost too vivid for me to see. They're
normal and everyday and usual, and I'm
the one who's different now. I am the
sunshine, that yellow streak I chased
as a nine-year-old. I dart faster than
a cartoon character across the screen,

leaving a little smoke or vapour trail puffing out behind me. But just for an instant. Now it feels like life is too crisp. Too sharp. I wonder if I can handle it this way, and the instant the wondering passes from my brain to my thought, I am finished realizing it was ever there. It occurs to me that life was supposed to be like this all along. Is this the way most normal people feel and think and live all the time? Can't be. They'd be too excited all the time to sit still! I can't sit here anymore. I have to jump, bounce, show what's going on inside. But I can't make you feel it with me. It's impossible. Ginny looks like she thinks I'm more crazy than ever. Even Joan the therapist doesn't truly believe me. What's the matter with you people? I must be on another planet. I've been zapped to an entirely new earth, a new body of land where I only have to think of something and it appears. No, that's not even it. There are no human words I am aware of to describe what's going on, describe it so you'd know what I think and feel, hear and think, anymore. There is just no way I can tell you because you can't think the way I do now. I'm the only one of me, the only one alive who can decipher what is going on in my brain.'

When I was eight, you said to me:
'In your whole body you haven't
the brains that Herbie has
in his little finger.'
When I was ten, you sucked my little breast.

When I was eleven, you said to me:
'You know I wouldn't do anything
to hurt you, honey.'
When I was twelve, you jammed
your fingers up inside me.

When I was twelve, you said to me:
'You liked that, didn't you, Diane?'
When I was thirteen, you
raped me from behind.

When I was twenty-eight, you said to me:
'I gave you a lesson in sex education.'
When I was forty-five, you broke my
mother's spine. When I was forty-six
She left you.

A Mother gives birth
Not to her child but to
her Salvation.
It matters only that her child
lives and breathes to give the Mother
credibility –
to make The Mother count.

A Father gives his seed
Not to his child but to
his Property.
It matters only that his child
can be fondled and abused to give the Father
satisfaction –
to make the Father powerful.

A brother discovers
Not a sister but
his Rescuer.
It matters only that his sister
is there when his needs call to give the Brother
sanctuary –
to make the Brother comfortable.

I have lost
my mother, my father, my brother.
My Bloodlines. My roots.
My entire Pretend Family.

I shall miss them only in my mind.
My heart already knew they were
never there.

I was orphaned
before I was conceived.

There is no dark no brown no shadows
everybody else sees the dark colours
I see only bright; only the perfect opposite of
filth. My blinders are gone.
Humans don't have words for this new vision I have
and I alone am responsible
for my new senses;
I made them
I invented them
I want to share them but
No one else is able to see them.
No one else is ready to see them.
It is enough that I have them.
I am all alone here but not lonely
Satisfied. Full. then Empty –
only washed, and cleaned, and sparkling Empty
My grin gives me away. Most people call this High,
Blown Away.
They're wrong – mistaken.
It's simply *being here* for the first time
when you've spent
50 years nowhere.

This isn't profound, please don't label it such –
This poem is the only way I know
to help you feel
me.

I look at the centre of Life
and tempt fate. Reckless.
Daring. Fearless?

Never fearless. I inch forward,
Together with Fears. Teamed up
with fears. No longer my enemy,
Fears tamed are my allies. Life
isn't safe from me now, I march

into its middle head-on, deliberate,
Determined to have You

Life   I choose Life
            I pursue Life
            I've missed You, Life.

Before I knew we could be friends,
I missed you. Fifty-four years
aching to touch
        to stroke
        to love   You.   Life.

Shall I weep and wail and strike out
at a world so cruel to us? Shall I
mourn for our years apart? Spend
our time together in sorrow?

Sorrow?
I feel none.
I search my heart over, and find not
one regret to whittle away our today.

For Ella Edwards Howard, 18 May, 1914 – 17 March, 1998

Our journey together has spanned fifty-seven years and I've just walked through them in nine days. The hard times. The stuff I didn't want to see again. Before I sat here with you, I couldn't have recited one good memory. As I watched and waited, I didn't find one good part.

Last week I was angry at the world and the people in it who led you to the pain and abuse you've lived. 'It ain't fair' was my theme and lament. Eighty-three years of abuse by father, husband, sons. Yours was an uncensored and uncensoring life. And I hated you for that. Why couldn't you see how people were using you? Why couldn't you leave your life of abuse? Why couldn't you let me rescue you?

Yesterday I wondered why you had to suffer so long to die. Today, putting this on paper, my eyes are opening. Now I know why you needed this much time to leave me – you still had more to teach.

You had to teach me that it's worth it to be a little too humble. That it's worth it to love a bit too much. That it's worth it to leave yourself too open to hurts and slights, because you're then open to love, caring, the joy of a rose, the smell of an ocean. You took too many hard knocks, but you gave joy to everyone you met. I think that is called a purpose in life.

Thanks, Mom. I always thought it would be an angry heart I'd carry, after all our struggles. Yours. Mine. Ours. What a surprise. A Mother who made mistakes, was all too human, has given me the ultimate gift: a whole new outlook on life, death, and everything in the middle. Suddenly I lament no more, blame no more, hate no more, weep no more. You are leaving me with a full heart.

Well, I guess I'm a slow learner, but here I am at last, Mom. You've given me the tools to continue my 'Life Education'. I promise to use them well and wisely. In your honour.

Written at my Mother's bedside when she was dying.

The true impact on victims of childhood abuse goes far beyond black eyes, bruises, sexual invasion and the desperation of daily living. The deepest scars are seldom seen or recognized. Author **Diane Ella Esther** has lived through and conquered the hopelessness that millions of abused children face daily. A frequent guest lecturer in universities, colleges and high schools, she conducts workshops for social workers, teachers, psychiatric practitioners and students. She provides a training and consulting service for sexual assault centres, women's shelters, adult and adolescent offenders' treatment centres, therapists and their clients – those adults whose childhoods were marred by sexual, physical, emotional abuse and neglect.

Ms. Esther writes an interactive weekly newspaper column entitled: 'Speaking of Abuse …' and is currently working on a comprehensive self-help guide book for abuse survivors, their partners, and their counsellors. She lives with her son Mark on Vancouver Island.

'Diane's work is like Diane herself: powerful. Her audiences are held spellbound. Diane serves as a potent reminder of the value of breaking the silence.' – *Suzanne Mulligan*, Coordinator, Community Child Abuse Council of Hamilton-Wentworth

'*Out of Incest & Abuse* will touch your heart, make you angry and give you hope. It is the story of the horror and the healing shared by survivors of childhood sexual abuse everywhere.' – *Mary Armstrong*, M.S.W., C.S.W., A.A.M.F.T., Psychotherapist, Toronto